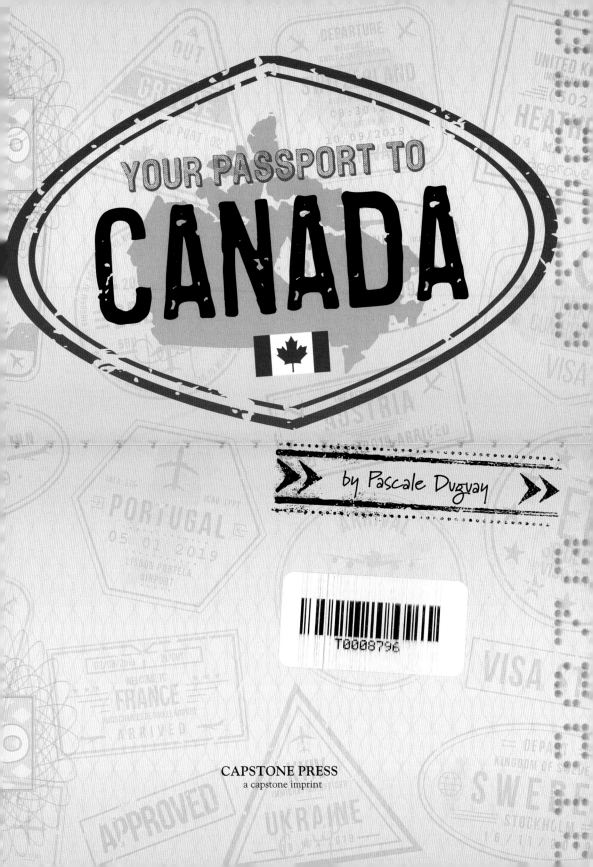

YOUR PASSPORT TO

CANADA

by Pascale Duguay

CAPSTONE PRESS
a capstone imprint

Published by Capstone Press, an imprint of Capstone
1710 Roe Crest Drive, North Mankato, Minnesota 56003
capstonepub.com

Library of Congress Cataloging-in-Publication Data is available on the Library
of Congress website.
ISBN: 9781669058380 (hardcover)
ISBN: 9781669058335 (paperback)
ISBN: 9781669058342 (ebook PDF)

Summary: What is it like to live in or visit Canada? What makes Canada's
culture unique? Explore the geography, traditions, and daily lives of Canadians.

Editorial Credits
Editor: Carrie Sheely; Designer: Bobbie Nuytten; Media Researcher: Rebekah
Hubstenberger; Production Specialist: Whitney Schaefer

Image Credits
Alamy: gary corbett, 16, North Wind Picture Archives, 9; Associated Press:
Nathan Denette/The Canadian Press, 23; Capstone Press: Eric Gohl, 5;
Dreamstime: Georgia Evans, 14; Getty Images: George Rose, 7, Hulton
Archive, 10, iStock/Barna Tanko, 15, iStock/jimfeng, 24, Justin Edmonds,
29, manonallard, 21, Tonda MacCharles/Toronto Star, 19, Vaughn Ridley,
27; Shutterstock: Art Babych, 13, beaulaz, 20, David P. Lewis, 17, Vlad G, 25,
Yunsun_Kim, Cover

Design Elements
Getty Images: iStock/Yevhenii Dubinko; Shutterstock: Flipser, Gil C, Net
Vector, pingebat, stas11

Printed and bound in China. PO 5593

CONTENTS

Words in **bold** are in the glossary.

CHAPTER ONE

WELCOME TO CANADA!

A wall of water crashes down Horseshoe Falls. A boat facing the falls is filled with tourists wearing rain ponchos. A mist from the falls sprays them. They admire the natural beauty around them.

Horseshoe Falls is a popular place to visit. It is located in two cities. Both cities are named Niagara Falls. Each city is on opposite sides of the border separating Canada and the United States. Horseshoe Falls is one waterfall of Niagara Falls on the Niagara River.

Canada and the United States are neighbors. They share the longest land border in the world. Canada is the second largest country after Russia.

Canada has different types of landscapes. They include mountains, grasslands, forests, and flat areas called **tundra**. There are also many rivers and lakes.

MAP OF CANADA

CANADA

Wood Buffalo
National Park

Vancouver
Banff
National Park
Lake Louise
Writing-on-Stone
Provincial Park

Montreal

OTTAWA

Toronto
CN Tower
Niagara Falls
Niagara River
Horseshoe
Falls

■ Capital City

● City

⬡ Landform

▲ Landmark

■ Park

N
W   E
S

Explore Canada's
cities and landmarks.

FACT FILE

OFFICIAL NAME: ....CANADA
POPULATION: 39,566,248
LAND AREA: .... 3,855,103 SQ. MI. (9,984,670 SQ KM)
CAPITAL: ....OTTAWA
MONEY: ....CANADIAN DOLLAR
GOVERNMENT: ....FEDERAL PARLIAMENTARY DEMOCRACY
LANGUAGE: ....ENGLISH AND FRENCH
GEOGRAPHY: Canada is in North America. It shares a border with the United States to the south and northwest. It is surrounded by the Pacific Ocean to the west, the Atlantic Ocean to the east, and the Arctic Ocean to the north.
NATURAL RESOURCES: Canada has oil, natural gas, coal, and hydroelectricity. It also has minerals such as gold, iron, uranium, copper, and nickel. Other natural resources include potash and lumber.

PEOPLE OF CANADA

Canada has more than 39 million people. It has a small population for its size. Most people live in the south. Fewer people live in the north. It is very cold there for much of the year.

Canada has two official languages. They are English and French. Most people who speak French live in the **province** of Quebec.

People in Vancouver, Canada, pose for a picture during a celebration.

People in Canada come from different backgrounds. **Indigenous** people have lived in Canada since ancient times. They make up about five percent of Canada's population. The Inuit live in northern **Arctic** areas. Many other Indigenous people live in Ontario, British Columbia, and Alberta.

Many Canadians have British, French, or Scottish backgrounds. **Immigrants** from all over the world also live in Canada.

CHAPTER TWO

HISTORY OF CANADA

Historians think that the first people who came to Canada were the Paleo-Indians. They arrived in Canada in about 10,000 BCE. They might have crossed a land bridge that used to connect Asia and North America. They also could have come by boat following the coast. The Paleo-Indians traveled through present-day Alaska and Yukon. Then they moved south. The Paleo-Indians were hunters. They followed herds of large animals such as mammoths and bison.

The Clovis people lived in Canada from about 9500 to 9000 BCE. Their tools were found in Yukon, Ontario, and Nova Scotia. They used spears with stone points for hunting. They also used stone scrapers to clean animal hides for clothing.

Paleo-Indians hunted for elk, deer, and other animals.

In 1759, the British led a successful attack on the city of Quebec during the Seven Years' War.

In the 1500s, British and French explorers began to arrive. They hoped to find gold and other riches. They didn't find gold. But animal furs, fish, and timber became valuable. Both the British and the French set up **colonies**.

The British and French started to fight each other with the help of the Indigenous people. Both sides wanted control of the land and its natural resources.

The last war between the British and French was called the Seven Years' War. The British won in 1763.

The British set aside land for the Indigenous people. But soon more Europeans arrived, and they wanted farmland. The British gave them a large part of the land belonging to Indigenous people. Many Indigenous people ended up with small areas of land called reserves.

FACT

In the 1600s, the fur trade became an important business in Canada. People shipped beaver furs to Europe to make felt hats.

TIMELINE OF CANADIAN HISTORY

ABOUT 10,000 BCE: Paleo-Indians come to Canada.

ABOUT 9500 TO 9000 BCE: The Clovis people live in Canada.

1021 CE: Vikings from Scandinavia settle briefly in L'Anse aux Meadows, Newfoundland.

1497: John Cabot, an Italian explorer, claims Newfoundland for England.

1534-1542: French explorer Jacques Cartier makes three voyages along the St. Lawrence River to claim land for France.

1600s: The French and British set up colonies in North America.

1756-1763: The British and French fight in the Seven Years' War. The British win.

1812-1814: In the War of 1812, Americans invade Canada but fail.

1867: Canada officially becomes a country made up of four provinces.

1999: The territory of Nunavut forms. Canada now has 10 provinces and three territories.

In 1840, there were three British territories in North America. These were the provinces of Canada, New Brunswick, and Nova Scotia. The British decided to join these territories to make one country. The province of Canada was split into two. It became the provinces of Ontario and Quebec. These two provinces joined Nova Scotia and New Brunswick to become the country of Canada in 1867. By 1999, Canada had 10 provinces and three territories.

The prime minister governs Canada. Every four years, elections are held. Canadians elect people to fill the seats in the House of Commons. The leader of the political party that wins the most seats usually becomes the prime minister. There is no limit to how many times a person can be prime minister. In 2015, Justin Trudeau became the prime minister.

Justin Trudeau

CHAPTER THREE

EXPLORE CANADA

Canada has many natural reserves and parks. The largest is Wood Buffalo National Park. It protects the nesting area of whooping cranes. These **migrating** birds are at risk of dying out. The park is also home to wood bison. It has the largest free-roaming herd in the world. Beavers in the park built a dam that can be seen from space.

FACT

Whooping cranes are the tallest birds in North America. Males can measure up to 5 feet (1.5 meters) tall. They have wingspans of 7.5 feet (2.3 m).

Peaks of the Canadian Rockies mountain range surround Lake Louise.

Canada has the most lakes in the world. Lake Louise in Banff National Park attracts many visitors. A **glacier** feeds the lake. Its stunning blue water comes from fine particles of rock that came off the glacier. The particles are called rock flour. Some of the rock flour floats beneath the surface. The sunlight reflects it.

A BIG CITY

Toronto has the largest population of any Canadian city. A popular attraction is the CN Tower. It is 1,815 feet (553 m) tall. It is the tallest tower in the Western **Hemisphere**. People can walk on the outside edge near the top while tied to a harness.

Prince Edward Island is Canada's smallest province. Some of its beaches have white sand, and others have red sand. The sand on Basin Head Beach is called singing sand. It makes a noise when you rub your feet in it.

The minerals in the sand at Basin Head Beach help make the unusual sounds.

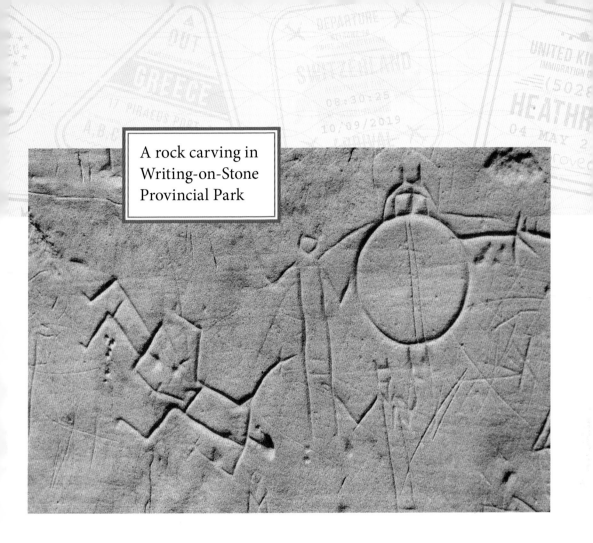

A rock carving in Writing-on-Stone Provincial Park

Visitors can learn about Indigenous **cultures** at places across Canada. In British Columbia, the Haida display their canoes at the Haida Heritage Centre. At the Wanuskewin Heritage Park in Saskatchewan, the Cree offer **tepees** to sleep in. In Writing-on-Stone Provincial Park in Alberta, people can see ancient carvings and paintings on sandstone cliffs. People of the Blackfoot Confederacy made the carvings and paintings.

CHAPTER FOUR
DAILY LIFE

Most Canadians live in cities. Some people who live in rural areas are farmers. They grow many types of grains, fruits, and vegetables. They also raise animals for meat, dairy products, and eggs. About 200,000 people live in the cold regions of the Arctic.

Children are required to go to school. They can start primary school as early as 4 years old. They finish high school at ages 17 or 18. Children can attend schools where people speak English or French. Public schools are free. Most don't require children to wear uniforms.

Immigrants make up almost one quarter of Canada's population. In 2021, most immigrants were born in Asia and the Middle East. Many people who recently immigrated to Canada live in large cities. Some open restaurants. People can taste dishes from all around the world in Toronto, Montreal, and Vancouver.

Children read at a school in Nunavut, Canada.

FOOD

Maple syrup is very popular. People in the province of Quebec produce the most maple syrup in the country. In early spring, people visit sugar shacks where maple syrup is made.

Other popular Canadian foods include poutine and beaver tails. Poutine is fries and cheese curds covered in gravy. Beaver tails are flat pieces of fried dough covered with sweet or savory toppings. For dessert, many Canadians enjoy Nanaimo bars. They have three layers made with a crumb base, vanilla custard, and melted chocolate.

Beaver tails

A sugar shack in Quebec

BAKED APPLES WITH MAPLE SYRUP

In Canada, apple picking is a popular fall activity. This recipe can be enjoyed as a snack or dessert. If you don't have maple syrup, you can use another type of sweet syrup.

Baked Apple Ingredients:
- 4 medium apples
- ¼ cup raisins
- ¼ cup brown sugar
- ½ teaspoon cinnamon
- 1 cup maple syrup

Baked Apple Directions:

1. Preheat oven to 350°F.
2. Core the apples with the help of an adult.
3. Place the apples in an 8- by 8-inch baking dish with the top holes facing up.
4. In a bowl, mix the raisins, brown sugar, and cinnamon.
5. Fill the apple holes with the raisin mixture.
6. Pour the maple syrup over the apples.
7. Bake for 30 to 35 minutes until the apples are soft.

CHAPTER FIVE
HOLIDAYS AND CELEBRATIONS

Canadians enjoy festivals and holidays. Many events include dancing, music, food, and games. Holidays include New Year's Day on January 1, Labour Day on the first Monday of September, and Thanksgiving on the second Monday in October. Christmas is on December 25.

Canada celebrates National Indigenous Peoples Day on June 21. It honors the country's three Indigenous groups. They are the First Nations, Inuit, and Métis. More than 630 communities make up the First Nations group.

FACT
The word *Inuit* means "the people" in the Inuit language.

On July 1, people celebrate Canada Day. It marks the day different territories joined to become the country of Canada in 1867. People gather to watch parades, concerts, and fireworks.

Singers perform on National Indigenous Peoples Day in Mississauga.

FESTIVALS

Major festivals take place around the country each season. In spring, the city of Ottawa in Ontario holds the Canadian Tulip Festival. Every April and May, visitors can see almost 1 million tulips. Some tulips are a gift from the Netherlands. They give the tulips to thank Canada for helping them during World War II (1939–1945).

Tulips bloom near a pond during the Canadian Tulip Festival in Ottawa.

In summer, the city of Halifax in Nova Scotia has the Busker Festival. Street performers entertain crowds. People can watch acrobats, magicians, and other performers.

In October, the Jasper Dark Sky Festival is held in Alberta. People gather to gaze at the stars. They can learn about space and do science activities.

Each February, the city of Quebec holds its Winter Carnival. It is one of the world's largest winter festivals. There are ice sculptures, canoe races, and parades.

People compete in canoe races at the Winter Carnival in Quebec.

CHAPTER SIX

SPORTS AND RECREATION

Schoolchildren take part in sports during gym class. They play many sports, including soccer, basketball, and badminton. Canada has two official national sports. They are ice hockey for winter and lacrosse for summer.

Canadians play hockey year-round for fun and on organized teams. People play the sport outside on ice, snow, pavement, or dirt. They also play it indoors in arenas and gyms. When it is played inside on surfaces with no ice, it is called floor hockey.

There are 32 teams in the National Hockey League (NHL). Twenty-five teams are in the United States. Canada has seven hockey teams in the NHL. Some of these teams are the Montreal Canadiens, Toronto Maple Leafs, and Edmonton Oilers. But almost half of the NHL's players are from Canada.

Montreal Canadiens goaltender Carey Price stops a shot from Toronto Maple Leafs forward John Tavares in an NHL game.

STICKS

Sticks is a game from the people of the Blackfoot Confederacy. Many of these Indigenous people live in Alberta. They are one of Canada's First Nations communities.

1. Divide players into two teams. Divide the playing area in half to make two territories.
2. Each team places four sticks in their territory. Now only players on the opposing team can touch the sticks.
3. Players try to capture the opposing team's sticks without getting tagged.
4. If players are tagged, they must sit until a teammate tags them back into the game. Then both get to walk safely back to their territory.
5. If players get tagged while holding a stick, they must put it back. When a stick is captured, it can't be taken back by the other team.
6. The team that captures all four sticks from the opposing team wins the game.

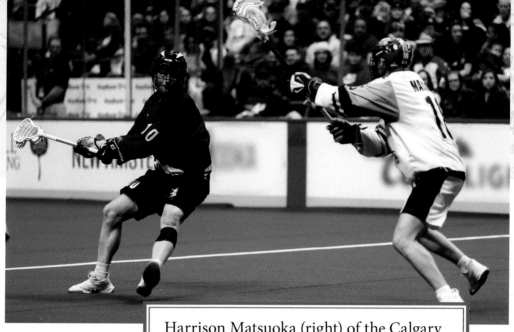

Harrison Matsuoka (right) of the Calgary Roughnecks and Rhys Duch (left) of the Colorado Mammoth play in an NLL game.

Indigenous people invented lacrosse in the 1300s or 1400s. Canadian teams are part of the National Lacrosse League (NLL). In 2022, more than half of the players in the NLL were from Canada. Many Canadian players are also in the Premier Lacrosse League (PLL).

A PLACE OF NATURAL BEAUTY

Canada is a country of amazing landscapes, beautiful parks, and abundant wildlife. Its people come from a wide range of cultures. Canada has much to offer the millions of tourists who visit the country each year.

GLOSSARY

Arctic (ARK-tik)
the area near the North Pole; the Arctic is cold and covered with ice

culture (KUHL-chuhr)
a people's way of life, ideas, art, customs, and traditions

glacier (GLAY-shur)
a huge moving body of ice found in mountain valleys or polar regions

hemisphere (HEM-uhss-fihr)
one half of Earth

immigrant (IM-uh-gruhnt)
someone who comes from one country to live permanently in another country

Indigenous (in-DI-juh-nuhs)
a way to describe the first people who lived in a certain area

province (PROV-uhnss)
a district or a region of some countries

tepee (TEE-pee)
a conical tent made by some Indigenous people

tundra (TUHN-druh)
a cold area of northern Europe, Asia, and North America where trees do not grow; the ground stays frozen in the tundra for most of the year

READ MORE

Birmingham, Maria. *Canada Wild: Animals Found Nowhere Else on Earth*. Halifax, Nova Scotia: Nimbus Publishing Limited, 2022.

Gould, Sloane, and Sharon Gordon. *Canada*. New York: Cavendish Square, 2023.

Kylie, Aaron. *Canada for Kids: 1000 Awesome Facts*. Buffalo, NY: Firefly Books, 2020.

INTERNET SITES

Canadian Geographic: Animal Facts: Wood Bison
canadiangeographic.ca/articles/animal-facts-wood-bison

Kiddle: Canada Facts for Kids
kids.kiddle.co/Canada

Wonderopolis: Where Is the Great White North?
wonderopolis.org/wonder/where-is-the-great-white-north

INDEX

ABOUT THE AUTHOR

Pascale Duguay writes for both children and adults on all sorts of fun topics. Her work has been published in Canada, the United States, and the United Kingdom. She also works as a school librarian where she loves to share her passion for reading.

SELECT BOOKS IN THIS SERIES